Explode The Code 6 1/2

Nancy Hall

EDUCATORS PUBLISHING SERVICE
Cambridge and Toronto

Cover design by Hugh Price

Printed in U.S.A.
ISBN 0-8388-1790-4
978-0-8388-1790-2

5 6 7 CUR 10 09 08

CONTENTS

Lesson 1

ar says /ar/ as in st**ar.** Read, write, and X it.			
1. archery archery			
2. parka __________			
3. parade __________			
4. starfish __________		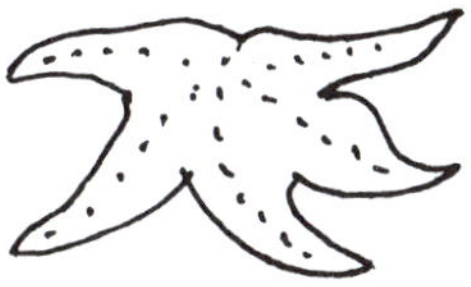	
5. carving __________			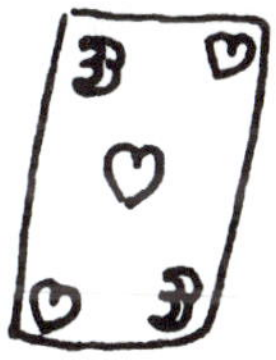
6. starting __________			
7. sparkle __________			

 it.

 partner or parking?	 party or sparkle?
 cartwheel or cabinet?	 harmful or shameful?
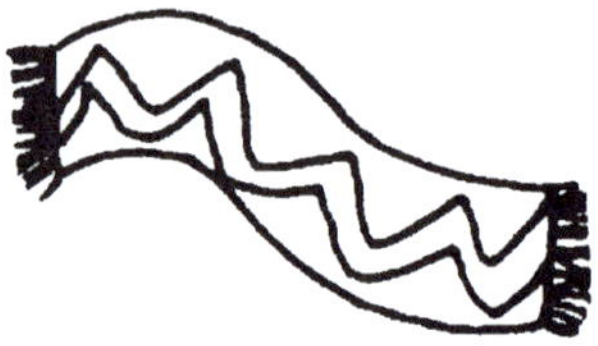 scar or scarf?	 barnyard or barrette?
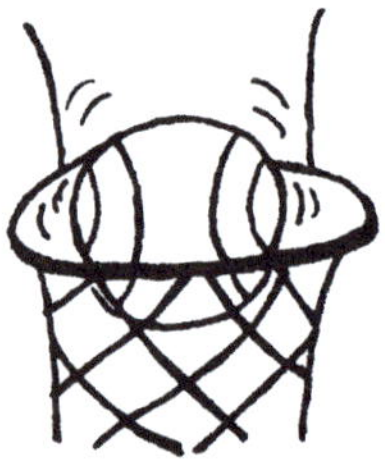 barbershop or basketball?	 carpet or carpenter?
 argument or ailment?	 marmalade or marched?

	Spell.		Write.
1.	 gar (car)	bet (pet)	carpet
2.	 spar star	kle fish	______
3.	 par char	coal ate	______
4.	 car cra	ving fin	______
5.	 bark brak	ling ing	______
6.	 mark nar	ers res	______
7.	 pra gar	pen den	______

Yes, no, or maybe?

		Yes	No	Maybe
1.	Can you put a starfish in a cardboard carton?	☒	☐	☐
2.	Will you loan your parka to your partner?	☐	☐	☐
3.	Can a carpenter make a marble bench?	☐	☐	☐
4.	Will you get markers at the hardware store?	☐	☐	☐
5.	Is it charming to have an argument at a party?	☐	☐	☐
6.	Will you starve if you eat marshmallows and marmalade?	☐	☐	☐
7.	Can you arrive too late for a carnival?	☐	☐	☐

 it.

 partner parking partly	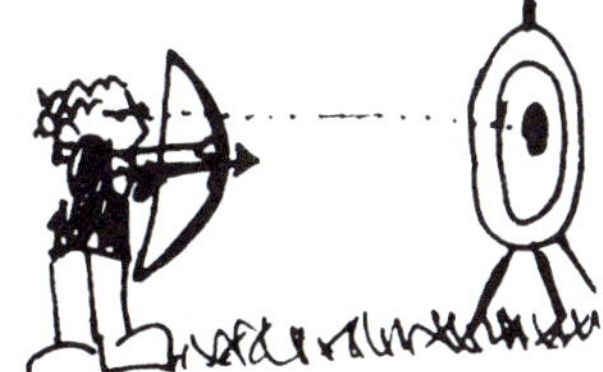 charter arctic archery
 markers market carving	 argument armful arching
 charcoal carton carnival	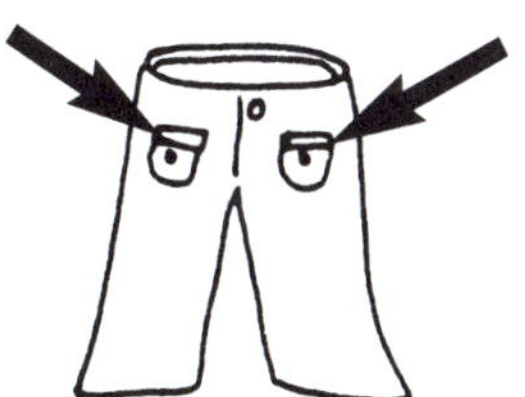 pockets parka partner
 framer farmer farther	 starving starring starling
 careful cards carton	 market marvel marbles

Pick the best word to finish each sentence.

sparkles	parka	starfish
parade	barking	arch
farther	garden	markers

1. That lovely ring sparkles in the sunshine.

2. She wore her red ________________ when she went skating.

3. Pluto is ________________ at the old dog in the car.

4. The ________________ is so lovely, leafy, and fragrant.

5. A ________________ is not a fish, but it is shaped like a star.

6. I ran ten miles, and I cannot run any ________________.

7. You can make a wonderful poster with cardboard and ________________.

X it.

1.
- The carpenter hit her finger by mistake. ☒
- The barber sticks his finger in the mustard. ☐

2.
- Arden starts the charcoal grill for supper. ☐
- Arden pulls so hard the grilled chop falls apart. ☐

3.
- Kareem starts to cry when he spills his milk. ☐
- Kareem spills the beans when he sees the witness. ☐

4.
- Omar watches the starting pitch at the ballpark. ☐
- The watch pinches Omar and makes his arm sore. ☐

5.
- Mark dreams he is rafting in the far Alps. ☐
- Marta can't go far from the tent in the darkness. ☐

6.
- Barb is staring at the marker in the road. ☐
- Barb is starting to bake pies for the market. ☐

7.
- Marty will be arrested for smashing into the parked truck. ☐
- March begins the spring season of rainy days. ☐

Write it, using a word with **ar.**

1.		sparkle
2.		
3.		
4.		
5.		
6.		
7.		

Lesson 2

or says /or/ as in f**or**k.

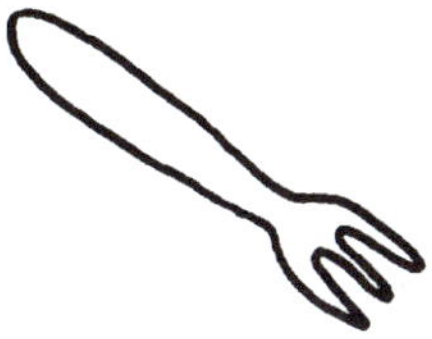

Read, write, and X it.

1.	gorilla ________			
2.	stormy ________	 Once upon a time there		
3.	orbit ________			
4.	shorter ________	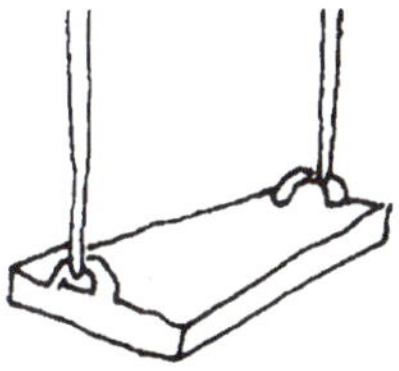		
5.	corn chips ________			
6.	porcupine ________			
7.	score ________	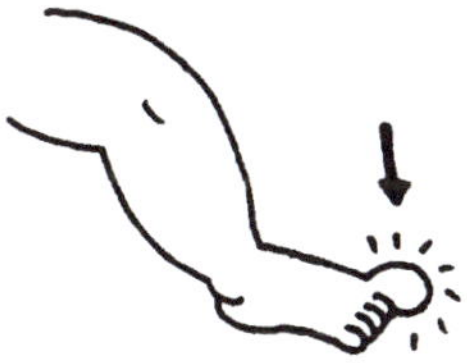	 HOME VISITOR 9 2	

 it.

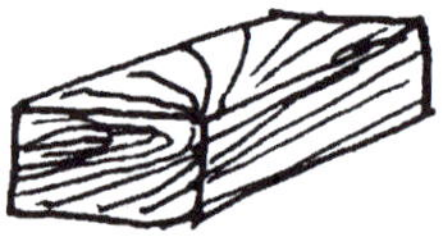 board or boring?	 sports car or sorted?
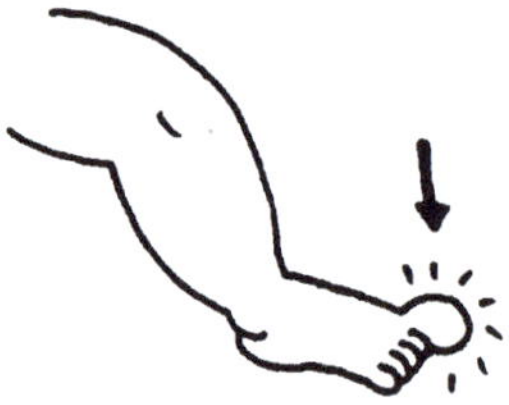 sorry or sore?	 florist or forest?
 horsefly or horseback?	 store or stare?
 odor or order?	 stock or stork?
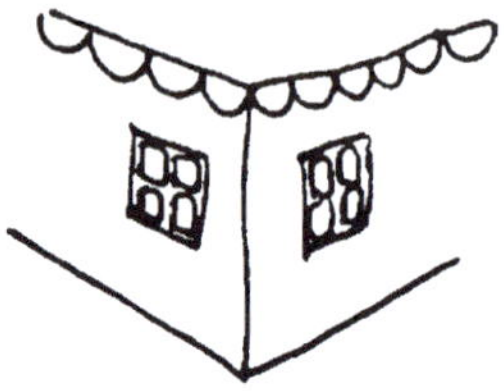 cornmeal or corner?	 corral or correct ?

	Spell.		Write.
1.	 bor snor	row ing	______________
2.	 or ro	per der	______________
3.	 shee sea	shore sore	______________
4.	 ar or	bit bor	______________
5.	 horse hose	back pack	______________
6.	 a ac	corns cons	______________
7.	 sort short	set er	______________

Yes, no, or maybe?

		Yes	No	Maybe
1.	Can you keep score at a game when you're at the seashore?	☐	☐	☐
2.	Is it an effort to write a story for homework?	☐	☐	☐
3.	When the forecast is perfect, is it stormy?	☐	☐	☐
4.	Do you like to eat cornflakes in the morning?	☐	☐	☐
5.	Is it correct to say twenty times twenty is forty?	☐	☐	☐
6.	Will a porcupine take a shortcut in the forest?	☐	☐	☐
7.	Can a gorilla order corn chips and garlic on the corner?	☐	☐	☐

◯ it.

boring
boarding
braiding
Once upon a time there
story
starry
stony
sharpen
snorkel
shortstop
tornado
torn
tomato
seashore
seahorse
seaside
armor
order
arbor
ignore
acorns
indoor
distort
dentist
doctor
corn cakes
corridor
cornflakes
oral
orbit
organ

Pick the best word to finish each sentence.

horseback porcupine acorn	doctor coral order	score stormy forgot

1. What was the final ______________ of the game?

2. A ______________ has sharp quills that can prick.

3. Teena needs to ______________ more cake for the party.

4. It is fun to ride ______________ on a sunny day.

5. An ______________ is a nut from an oak tree.

6. If you do not feel better, you must call the ______________.

7. It is best to play inside on a ______________ day.

X it.

1.
- Boris has forty morning glories in his garden. ☐
- Boris will be forty years old tomorrow morning. ☐

2.
- The kids can't afford to get Fido a hot dog. ☐
- The kids in the story take six dogs in a Ford. ☐

3.
- Doris wants to score a run in the baseball game. ☐
- The rest of the team is much shorter than Doris. ☐

4.
- I ride my horse to the harbor to catch crabs. ☐
- Flora orders a fishing pole from the store. ☐

5.
- We pass a bus of kids as we are riding horseback. ☐
- As Porky Pig passes the parked bus, a kid cheers. ☐

6.
- Morris gets a kick out of going to the store. ☐
- Morris kicks a bag of torn paper from the party. ☐

7.
- A hornet stung Becky and made her leg red and sore. ☐
- The seashore beacon helps boats into the harbor. ☐

Write it, using a word with **or.**

1.		______________________
2.		______________________
3.	HOME | VISITOR 9 | 2	______________________
4.		______________________
5.		______________________
6.		______________________
7.		______________________

Lesson 3

er, ir, ur, and sometimes **ear** say /er/
as in h**er,** b**ir**d, b**ur**n, and l**ear**n.

Read, write, and X it.

1. butterfly ______			
2. surprise ______			
3. hamburg ______			
4. thirsty ______			
5. perfume ______			
6. purse ______	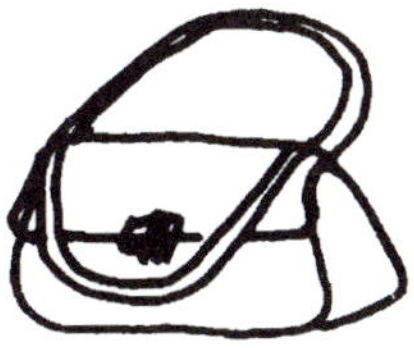		
7. learn ______			

◯ it.

sherbet or shiver?
student or stirring?
ladder or turban?
disturb or dirty?
turpentine or thirteen?
enter or embark?
temper or turnip?
overboard or overheard?
serpent or servant?
squirted or squirrel?

	Spell.		Write.
1.	tel let	ten ter	________________
2.	bol lob	ster ser	________________
3.	per par	son mit	________________
4.	stir sti	ring king	________________
5.	dir per	ty fume	________________
6.	bet but	tard ter	________________
7.	squirt quot	ed ep	________________

Yes, no, or maybe?

		Yes	No	Maybe
1.	Is perfume a better gift than a silver dollar?	☐	☐	☐
2.	Is it important to clean a paintbrush in turpentine?	☐	☐	☐
3.	Do you curtsy after you perform in church?	☐	☐	☐
4.	Will we disturb you if we chatter together?	☐	☐	☐
5.	Was it smart to turn to the back and read the ending first?	☐	☐	☐
6.	Would you leave your purse at the Safeway supermarket?	☐	☐	☐
7.	Is a surprise a perfect ending?	☐	☐	☐

 it.

 learning leaning leaving	 differ dinner dirty
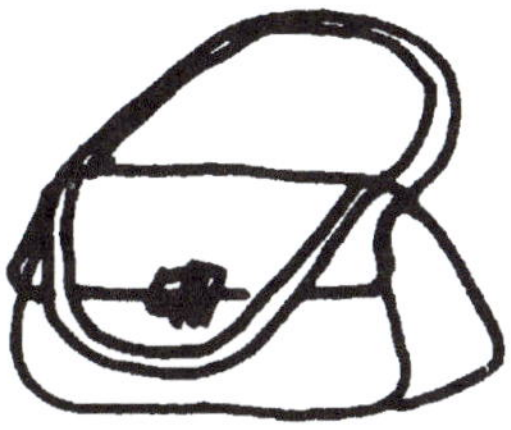 surplus purse surprise	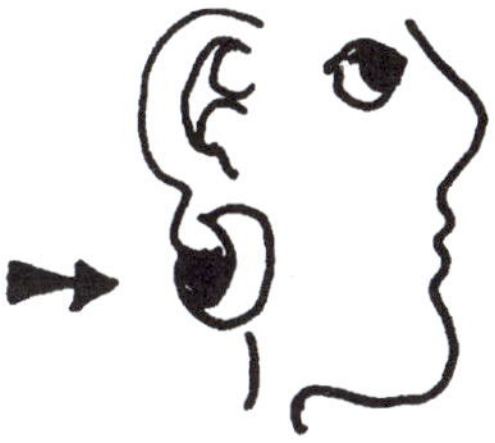 earth earring yearning
 turnip turtle turkey	 perform perhaps perfume
 sherbet serpent starlit	 whisker whisper witches
 early earnings earnest	 hamburg hamster humbug

Pick the best word to finish each sentence.

thirsty	purse	earthquake
butter	perfume	murder
learning	lobster	hamburg

1. Bernard is ____________________ how to swim.

2. A ____________________ has a hard shell and lives in the sea.

3. A ____________________ is useful for carrying small things.

4. You put ____________________ on toast, baked potato, and popcorn.

5. Running in the hot sun makes you feel ____________________.

6. For supper I like ____________________ on a bun with ketchup.

7. Her ____________________ smelled like a floral garden.

X it.

1.	Last Thursday a silly bird rode its bike into the traffic.	☐	
	Roberta is biking to the beach on Thursday.	☐	
2.	The carrots are growing taller than Jamal.	☐	
	Jamal is stirring carrots in the biggest bowl.	☐	
3.	We must hurry to class before the bell rings.	☐	
	Harry and Weng perform for the class.	☐	
4.	A serpent cannot carry a backpack.	☐	
	Carmen has a picnic with her pal, the serpent.	☐	
5.	The blackbird rakes the earth and plants a garden.	☐	
	The blackbird is eating insects in the garden.	☐	
6.	Shantal and her son collect pinecones.	☐	
	The hot sun starts to melt the sherbet cone.	☐	
7.	Burt picks a daisy as a surprise for Ahmed.	☐	
	Daisy makes a surprise visit to Bertha.	☐	

Write it, using a word with **er, ir, ur,** or **ear.**

1.	________________
2.	________________
3.	________________
4.	________________
5.	________________
6.	________________
7.	________________

Lesson 4

wor says /wer/ as in **wor**k.  **war** says /wor/ as in **war**m.

Read, write, and X it.

1.	fireworks ____________			
2.	workshop ____________			
3.	worship ____________			
4.	wormy ____________			
5.	warning ____________			
6.	award ____________			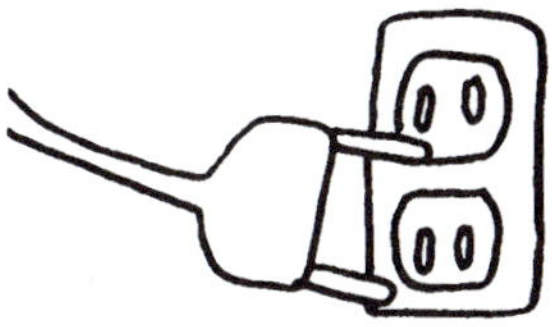
7.	warm-up ____________			

 it.

 warships or hardship?	 workshop or worship?
 homework or homeward?	 worn or swarm?
 worry or worship?	 worker or warrior?
 worthwhile or worthless?	 warm-up or workload?
 warfare or worst?	 warble or warmest?

	Spell.		Write.
1.	 home ward	robe work	______________
2.	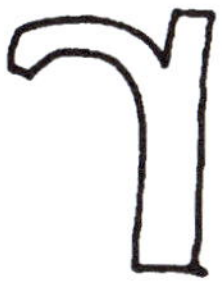 back pack	ward horse	______________
3.	 arm art	work worm	______________
4.	 war warm	plan er	______________
5.	 worm wart	et y	______________
6.	 in a	ward word	______________
7.	 fir fire	plane works	______________

Yes, no, or maybe?

		Yes	No	Maybe
1.	Is a wormy apple the worst?	☐	☐	☐
2.	Will you worry if you flunk the test?	☐	☐	☐
3.	Should you warm up before going to church?	☐	☐	☐
4.	Will you have fireworks in a birdbath?	☐	☐	☐
5.	Does a warbler have a wardrobe?	☐	☐	☐
6.	Can you get an award for the best sunburn?	☐	☐	☐
7.	Can you make a bird feeder in a workshop?	☐	☐	☐

 it.

award alarm aware	sunburn birdbath workbook
wormy wordy worldly	morning barking wearing
world worst worse	weeping warpath warthog
earwax earthworm earliest	firefly fireman fireworks
waterway wardrobe warbling	backward forward afterward

Pick the best word to finish each sentence.

warble	award	worthwhile
homework	worthy	warning
worship	warm-ups	backward

1. As the storm came closer to shore, a ___________________ was posted.

2. Have you ever heard a bluebird ___________________?

3. Can you jump rope ___________________ without falling?

4. Walter got the class ___________________ for being the best worker.

5. You must do some ___________________ before jogging five miles.

6. Too much ___________________ makes a student grumpy.

7. We go to church or temple to ___________________ .

X it.

1.	Gramp put bushels of wormy apples in his van.	☐	
	Granny's van is painted with wormy apples.	☐	
2.	Silvester slides down the railing backward.	☐	
	Silvester makes his train go backward in the dirt.	☐	
3.	Norma makes the worst racket when she sings.	☐	
	Norma makes a racket when she swats the hornet.	☐	
4.	Tomás wants to set up his artwork to show.	☐	
	Tomás wants to get a warm jacket for his puppy.	☐	
5.	Wally gets an award for winning the long jump.	☐	
	Wally is learning to juggle so he can win an award.	☐	
6.	Mariko's sneakers are worn out from jogging.	☐	
	Mariko feels worn out from chopping wood.	☐	
7.	Ping put her rowboat in the workshop.	☐	
	Ping needs to repair her car before work.	☐	

Write it, using a word with **wor** or **war.**

1.		____________________________________
2.		____________________________________
3.		____________________________________
4.		____________________________________
5.		____________________________________
6.	1st	____________________________________
7.	r	____________________________________

Lesson 5

igh says / ī / as in l**igh**t.

Read, write, and X it.

1.	nightmare ____________			
2.	sightsee ____________			
3.	firefighter ____________			
4.	light bulb ____________			
5.	tightrope ____________		 TAXI	
6.	stoplight ____________			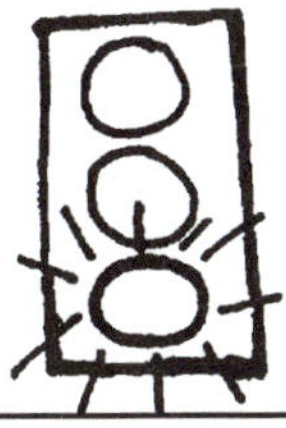
7.	highway ____________			

 it.

 jump rope or ringworm?	 flight or fright?
 nearsighted or sightseeing?	 nightfall or nightshirt?
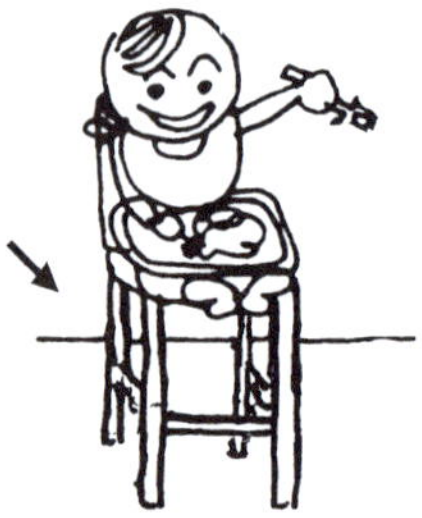 high chair or highway?	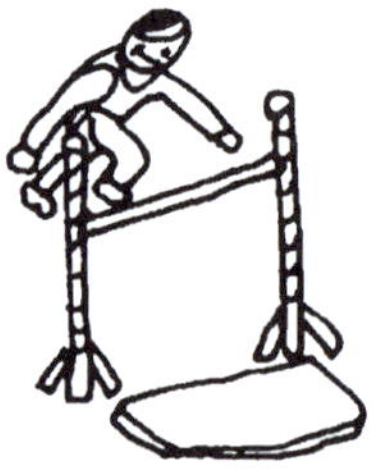 hijack or high jump?
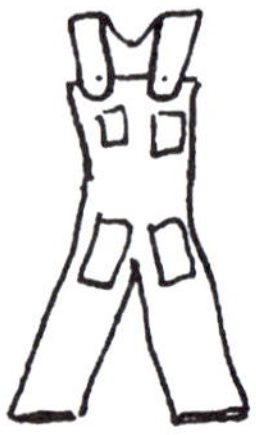 overnight or overalls?	 tightrope or twilight?
 stoplight or spotlights?	 fighter or frightful?

	Spell.		Write.
1.	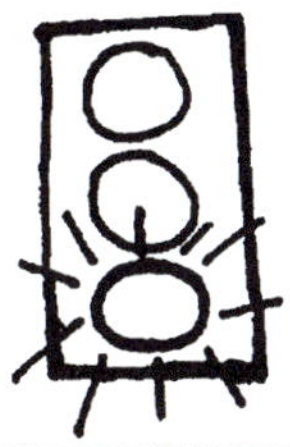 stop step	light high	____________
2.	 far fire	flight fighter	____________
3.	 high right	hand way	____________
4.	 late light	ent ning	____________
5.	 night tight	mare more	____________
6.	 hing high	way wade	____________
7.	 might sight	seed see	____________

Yes, no, or maybe?

		Yes	No	Maybe
1.	Will they use a spotlight in a show?	☐	☐	☐
2.	Are you a right-handed batter?	☐	☐	☐
3.	Can a high-speed sports car be out of sight?	☐	☐	☐
4.	Is a firefighter lighter than air?	☐	☐	☐
5.	Is it fun to stay overnight with a pal?	☐	☐	☐
6.	If you have glasses, are you nearsighted?	☐	☐	☐
7.	Can a nightmare be frightful?	☐	☐	☐

it.

 fire truck fireworks firefighter	 rightness brightest highness
 high-rise high chair high speed	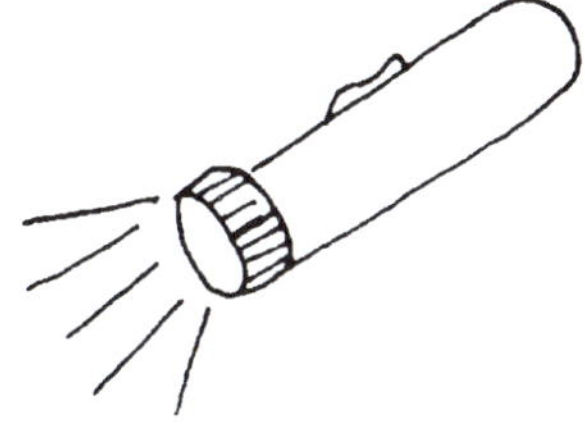 flashback flashlight twilight
 nightingale nighttime nightmare	 lightness relighted delighted
 lightning bug lightning lighter	 midnight daylight daydream
 right hand right on nearsighted	 fighting flightless frightened

Pick the best word to finish each sentence.

sightseeing	tightrope	brightest
firefighter	tonight	frightened
high-risk	nightshirt	lightning

1. Sky diving is a ____________________ sport.

2. The job of a ____________________ is also high risk.

3. I awoke when a bolt of ____________________ struck the tree.

4. We are going on a ____________________ trip in Vermont.

5. I undressed, put on my ____________________, and went to bed.

6. The ____________________ walker performed without a net.

7. Oscar is the ____________________ student in our class.

X it.

1.	Tom Cat drives slowly and stops at all the lights.	☐	
	The stoplight turned slowly from green to red.	☐	
2.	Darrell grabs a snowball with his right arm.	☐	
	The snowman grabs Darrell with his right hand.	☐	
3.	There was too much traffic on the highway.	☐	
	Tarik likes to jog on a highway without traffic.	☐	
4.	In Nita's nightmare her motorbike is junk.	☐	
	Nita rides her motorbike on the tightrope.	☐	
5.	If you sing like a bird, you must sing high.	☐	
	High in the tree, Rafe sings and plays his drum.	☐	
6.	Hilly is surprised that a queen needs a high chair.	☐	
	His Highness gives Hilly a big surprise.	☐	
7.	The brightest student in the class wins the award.	☐	
	That student has the brightest wardrobe.	☐	

Write it, using a word with **igh.**

1.	_______________
2.	_______________
3.	_______________
4.	_______________
5.	_______________
6.	_______________
7.	_______________

Lesson 6

oo says /o͞o/ as in b**oo**t and /o͝o/ as in b**oo**k.

Read, write, and X it.

1.	shook ______________			
2.	woodpecker ______________			
3.	rooster ______________			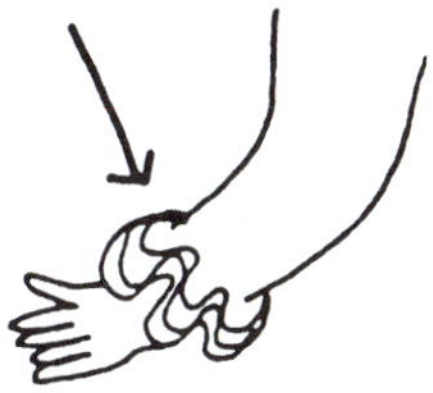
4.	workbook ______________			
5.	bedroom ______________			
6.	mushrooms ______________			
7.	fishhook ______________			

◯ it.

looking or hooking?
shoot or shook?
woodchuck or woodcutter?
booming or blooming?
raccoons or cocoons?
hoof or hood?
cookbook or cook pot?
barefooted or bamboo?
woolly or woody?
high school or school bus?
7

	Spell.		Write.
1.	 kanga roo	ster sten	______
2.	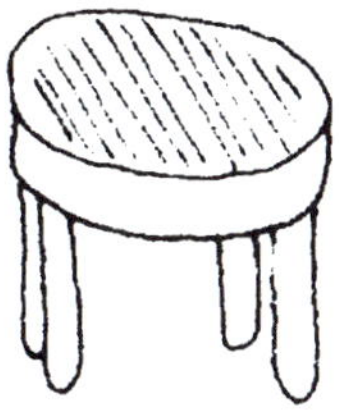 fool foot	stood stool	______
3.	 crook cook	ish ing	______
4.	 took tool	box fox	______
5.	 bell bal	loon loot	______
6.	 crook cook	ed er	______
7.	 leek look	est ing	______

Yes, no, or maybe?

		Yes	No	Maybe
1.	Will a woodpecker go barefooted?	☐	☐	☐
2.	Do you need footlights to make footprints?	☐	☐	☐
3.	Is it foolish to take a spoonful of marmalade at bedtime?	☐	☐	☐
4.	Can a moose play a woodwind in the band?	☐	☐	☐
5.	Will a baboon call from a phone booth?	☐	☐	☐
6.	Can you lose a rooster in the hen coop?	☐	☐	☐
7.	Can you take a footpath into the woodland?	☐	☐	☐

it.
footstool
footman
footloose
high-strung
schoolroom
high school
SALE
BESTSELLERS
bookends
bookstore
bookmark
woodcutter
workbook
woodpecker
caboose
kangaroo
cooler
scooping
scooter
snooping
cartoon
bedroom
bootees
poodle
poolroom
papoose
sloop
stoop
loop
understood
smooth
stood

Pick the best word to finish each sentence.

raccoon	mushrooms	football
woodpecker	toolbox	footstool
workbook	shook	balloon

1. Do you like ____________________ on your pizza?

2. When Gramp rests, he puts his feet on the ____________________.

3. We have homework tonight in our spelling ____________________.

4. The carpenter can carry his tools in a __________________.

5. The gray-and-black animal with a mask is a ____________________.

6. During the earthquake, the entire room ____________________.

7. At the birthday party we each got a big ____________________.

X it.

1.	Joan's foot slipped and she took a spill. ☐ Joan made a crooked footstool for the cook. ☐	
2.	Pablo has a smooth ride in the hot air balloon. ☐ The school bus did not have a smooth ride. ☐	
3.	Suki shook her rod and hooked a big fish. ☐ Rover lost his bone at the toll booth. ☐	
4.	Troody is cooling off the warm bathroom. ☐ Troody put a water cooler in the back room. ☐	
5.	Shamboo is too tired to find the school bus. ☐ Boo needs her toolbox to crank up the school bus tire. ☐	
6.	Yasmin is scooping out holes in the earth. ☐ Yasmin is scooping up frozen yogurt cones. ☐	
7.	Rudy has a pet woodpecker called Woody. ☐ Woody the woodcutter called from the forest. ☐	

Write it, using a word with **oo.**

1.

2.

3.

4.

5.

6.

7.

Lesson 7

ea has three sounds: Sometimes **ea** says /ē/ as in b**ea**ds. Sometimes **ea** says /ĕ/ as in h**ea**d. Sometimes **ea** says /ā/ as in gr**ea**t.

Read, write, and **X** it.

1.	steak ____________			
2.	peach ____________			
3.	pleasant ____________			
4.	sneakers ____________			
5.	underneath ____________			
6.	break ____________			
7.	sweating ____________			

 it.

 braver or beaver?	 pitch or peach?
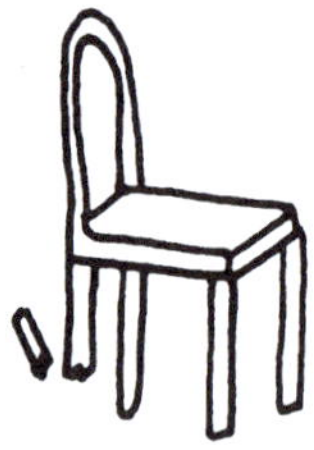 breakable or beef steak?	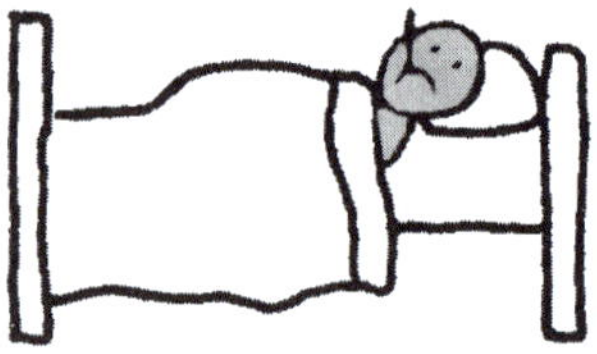 bad health or bad breath?
 sneaker or speaker?	 teammates or spearmint?
 beating or beacon?	 chess or treasure?
 breaded or breathless?	 heavy or head?

	Spell.		Write.
1.	 bea beet	ver gin	____________
2.	 head hea	vy ven	____________
3.	 ear ea	ger gle	____________
4.	 sweet sweat	er ing	____________
5. 1ft. 2ft. 3ft.	 meet mea	sure ing	____________
6.	 health heal	y le	____________
7.	 ultra under	neat neath	____________

Yes, no, or maybe?

		Yes	No	Maybe
1.	Is it pleasant to break your ankle?	☐	☐	☐
2.	Will the teammates elect a leader?	☐	☐	☐
3.	Is it dreadful to have fleas in the bedroom?	☐	☐	☐
4.	Do you say a prayer at mealtime?	☐	☐	☐
5.	Would you spread beach-plum jam on bread?	☐	☐	☐
6.	Does a beaver shave his beard in the morning?	☐	☐	☐
7.	Do you wear a headband on your forehead when you jog?	☐	☐	☐

(circle) it.

forehead
forward
forest

teapot
teacup
hiccup

whether
weather
wealthy

grateful
dreadful
dead end

leaking
leaning
leafy

cardboard
breadboard
boardroom

feathers
fearful
tearful

headband
headboard
headstrong

braided
bearded
breaded

lemonade
leotard
leapfrog

Pick the best word to finish each sentence.

break	beaver	sweatpants
underneath	headband	dreadful
heavy	peach	steak

1. Be careful of these old dishes; they will ____________ quite easily.

2. It is best to wear ____________ and a ____________ when jogging.

3. A ____________ can cut down trees with its teeth and build dams.

4. I will meet you ____________ the flagpole at the high school.

5. Sometimes we have grilled ____________ with mushrooms for dinner.

6. What is fuzzy on the outside and tasty on the inside? A ____________.

7. My book bag is so ____________ that I can hardly carry it home.

X it.

1.	Beazy has the bunk underneath her teammate.	☐	
	Tansy and her teammate both have fleas.	☐	
2.	Miranda beats the dreadful dragon.	☐	
	Miranda has a pleasant time at the beach.	☐	
3.	Terry gets a Band-Aid for the cut on his forehead.	☐	
	The bandleader needs to learn the tempo.	☐	
4.	Pedro is leaning back in his chair reading a book.	☐	
	After learning to do headstands, Pedro is sweating.	☐	
5.	Luisa is dreading the day when she will be leader.	☐	
	Hungry Luisa is dreaming about the next mealtime.	☐	
6.	The puppet has opened the treasure chest.	☐	
	The pupils are going on a treasure hunt.	☐	
7.	I can't bear bugs flying near my mug of tea.	☐	
	Shoshana was fearless when flying solo.	☐	

Write it, using a word with **ea.**

1.		______________________________
2.		______________________________
3.		______________________________
4.		______________________________
5.		______________________________
6.		______________________________
7.		______________________________

Lesson 8

ie and **ey** say /ē/ as in th**ie**f and k**ey**. Read, write, and X it.			
1. volleyball ___	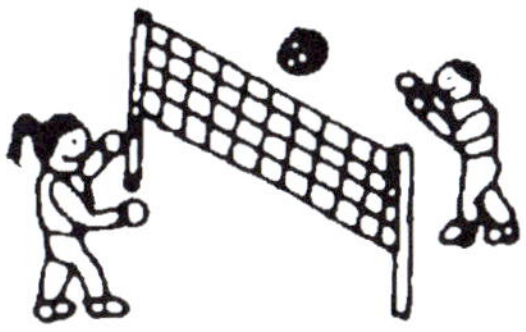		
2. honeybees ___			
3. handkerchief ___			
4. ballfield ___			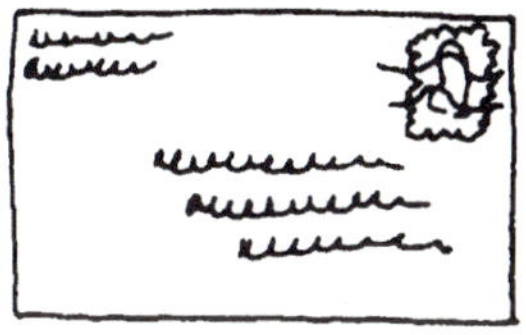
5. windshield ___			
6. jockey ___		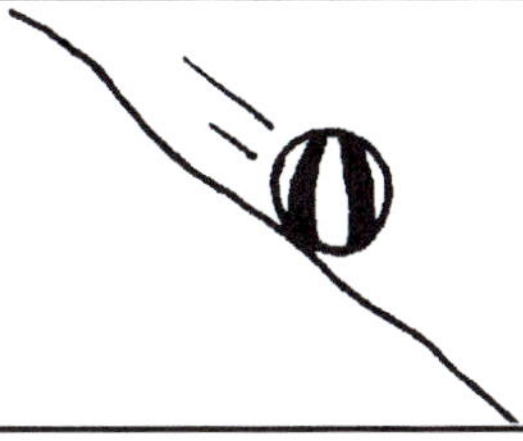	
7. briefcase ___			

 it.

 chimney or chummy?	 hockey stick or honeybees?
 monkey wrench or moneymaker?	 crooked or cookies?
 alley cat or bowling alley?	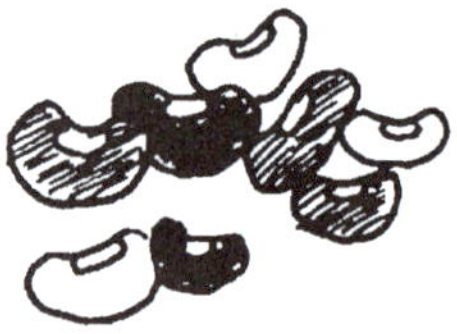 kidney beans or kidneys?
 moonshine or monkeyshines?	 right fielder or right-of-way?
 money bags or many bugs?	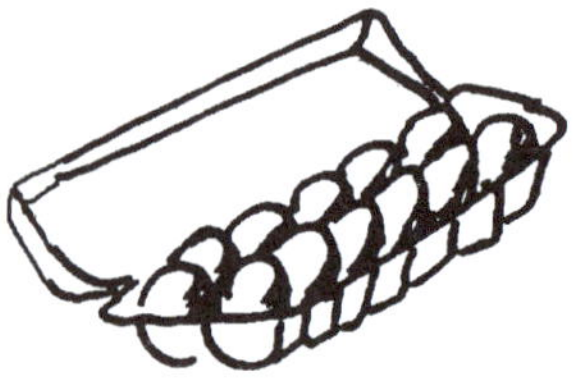 donkey or dozen?

	Spell.		Write.
1.	 shim chim	ney mer	______
2.	 cook look	ies ist	______
3.	 joc tur	key nip	______
4.	 beef brief	cast case	______
5.	 hick hock	er ey	______
6.	 aim ball	filed field	______
7.	 wall wind	ley shield	______

Yes, no, or maybe?

		Yes	No	Maybe
1.	Will a friend take you on her honeymoon?	☐	☐	☐
2.	Can a woodchuck shield you from honeybees?	☐	☐	☐
3.	Do you need a briefcase if you are a moneymaker?	☐	☐	☐
4.	Can a monkey be part of a volleyball team?	☐	☐	☐
5.	Do you like kidney beans and hamburg meat in chili?	☐	☐	☐
6.	Will a jockey use a hockey stick when he is riding?	☐	☐	☐
7.	Do you believe in monkeyshines and chimney sweeps?	☐	☐	☐

 it.

 altogether alligator alleyway	 shield shells sheet
 keyboard keystone keyhole	 honeysuckle hockey stick hockey goal
 chimney bully trolley	 valley walled valentine
 ballfield believe fielder	 parsley paisley partly
 moneylender mongrel monkish	 priest prefix piecrust

Pick the best word to finish each sentence.

ballfield	believe	chimney
cookies	jockey	brief
alley	windshield	honeybees

1. It is hard to ____________________ that today is the shortest day of the year.

2. A____________________ is usually a short person who handles horses well.

3. We will meet tonight at the ____________________ for the team play-off.

4. There was a swarm of ____________________ buzzing in the apple tree.

5. I like to have a glass of milk and some____________________ when I get home.

6. Santa and smoke both go up the ____________________.

7. When it rains we turn on the ____________________ wipers in the car.

X it.

1.
- Lisa uses a key to wind up the walking dog. ☐
- Lise gets keyed up when she has to walk the dog. ☐

2.
- Walt puts in his money to play the video game. ☐
- Making a wish, Walt throws his money in the well. ☐

3.
- The number-one jockey believes he can win. ☐
- The hockey player believes that she is number one. ☐

4.
- Mom takes Rupa and her briefcase to work. ☐
- Rupa takes Mom for a brief whirl on her bike. ☐

5.
- He needs steak, parsley, and cookies for dinner. ☐
- The monkey puts the cookies in the briefcase. ☐

6.
- A windshield is a great help to a driver. ☐
- Kenisha has great fun at the airfield. ☐

7.
- The umpire tells the left fielder to behave. ☐
- The vampire tells us to behave on the field trip. ☐

Write it, using **ie, ee,** or **ey.**

1. ____________________

2. ____________________

3. ____________________

4. ____________________

5. ____________________

6. ____________________

7. ____________________

Lesson 9

oi and **oy** say /oy/ as in b**oi**l and b**oy.**

Read, write, and X it.

1.	pointing ______________			
2.	salad oil ______________			
3.	pull toy ______________			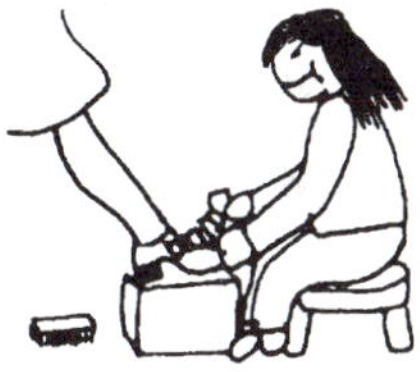
4.	joint ______________		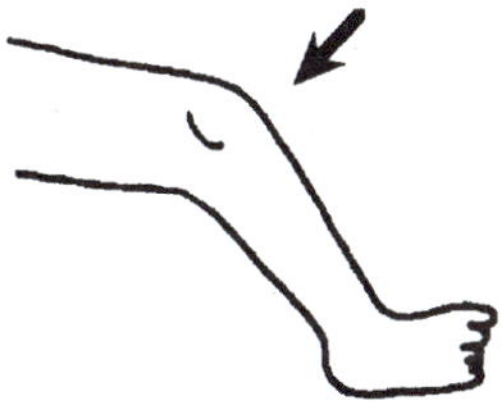	
5.	spoiled ______________			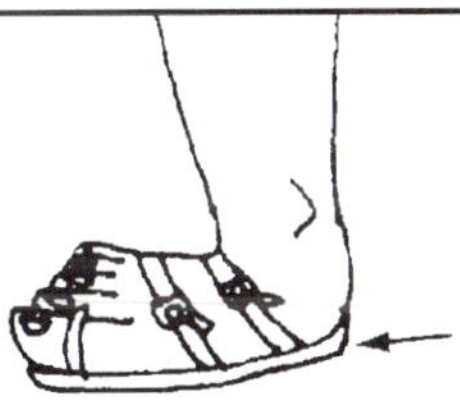
6.	moist ______________			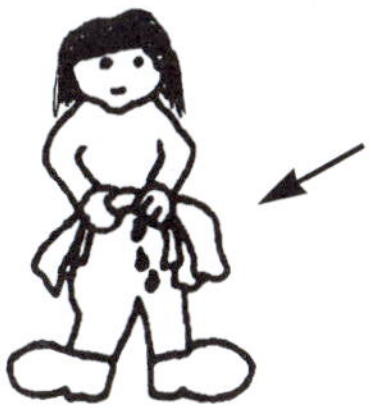
7.	sirloin steak ______________		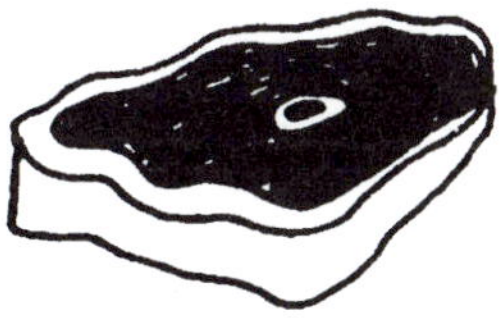	

 it.

 noisy or nosy?	 joyful or jellyfish?
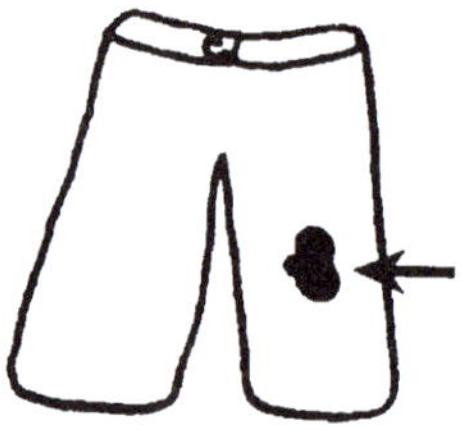 soybeans or soiled?	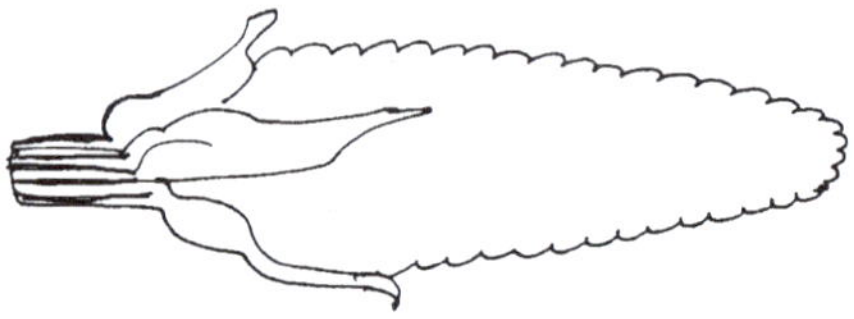 corn-on-the-cob or corduroy?
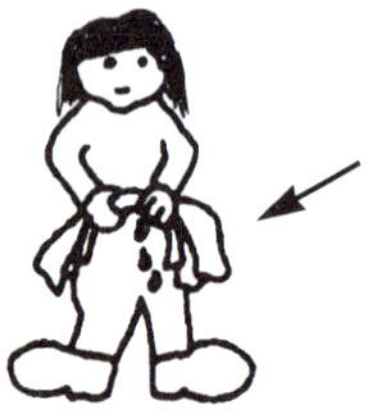 moose or moist?	 loyal or royal?
 spoiled or coiled?	 destroy or decoy?
 pontoon or poison?	 pointed hat or painting cap?

	Spell.		Write.
1.	 nor noi	sy ton	________
2.	 joy roy	al ful	________
3.	 oil oink	y end	________
4.	 poi boi	sent son	________
5.	 bowl broil	ert ing	________
6.	 point join	ing less	________
7.	 oy oil	ster man	________

Yes, no, or maybe?

		Yes	No	Maybe
1.	Will a noisy pig say, "Oink, oink"?	☐	☐	☐
2.	Will it annoy you if I put garlic in the salad oil?	☐	☐	☐
3.	Will a tiny baby enjoy a pull toy?	☐	☐	☐
4.	Is a hard-boiled egg poison?	☐	☐	☐
5.	Will a paperboy wear corduroy sweatpants in summer?	☐	☐	☐
6.	Do your joints feel painful when the air is moist?	☐	☐	☐
7.	Are you joyful when you must oil your bike?	☐	☐	☐

 it.

 bowling boiling broiling	 embroider embarrass envelope
 pull toy pulley overjoyed	 joking together joined hands jogged slowly
 coil coin cone	 sorted soiled sailed
 hosting hoisting roasting	 ointment appointment old-time
 tinfoil tenfold tin can	 ornery oily oyster

Pick the best word to finish each sentence.

noisy	poison	broiling
ointment	joyful	moist
pointing	oiling	coins

1. Beware of bottles with the word ____________________ on them.

2. The gatekeeper is ____________________ at the broken gate.

3. It was a ____________________ day when we won the big game.

4. Most of the time a dog's nose is cool and ____________________.

5. That squeaky door needs ____________________ .

6. The ____________________ cats kept us awake all night long.

7. There can be smoke when you are ____________________ meat.

X it.

1.	He mixed a very oily salad dressing. ☐ She mixed up the twins, Olive Oil and Vinny. ☐	
2.	Tess joined the same stamp club as Roy. ☐ Tess joined Roy in the archery contest. ☐	
3.	Toshy is pointing at the most wonderful cat. ☐ Toshy's wonderful pointed hat is quite moist. ☐	
4.	It can be annoying to hear a pig oinking. ☐ It can be annoying to hear oil dripping. ☐	
5.	Hal asks Her Royal Highness if he can be a paperboy. ☐ Hal gives Her Royal Highness a gold, coiled belt. ☐	
6.	Porky Pig is joyful to meet the prizefighter. ☐ Porky Pig is joyful to have won the grand prize. ☐	
7.	Dinesh takes the food and puts it away so it won't spoil. ☐ Dinah eats oysters and french fries at the takeout. ☐	

Write it, using a word with **oi** or **oy.**

1.		____________________
2.		____________________
3.		____________________
4.		____________________
5.		____________________
6.		____________________
7.	FIRE	____________________

Lesson 10

ou and sometimes **ow** say /ou/ as in m**ou**th and c**ow.**

Read, write, and X it.

1.	couch ____________		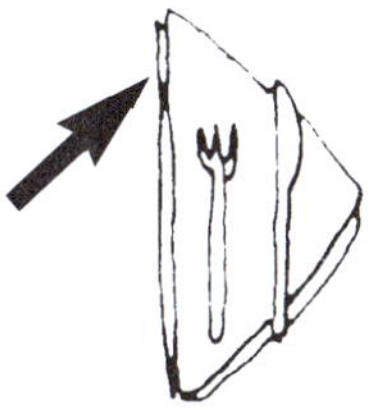	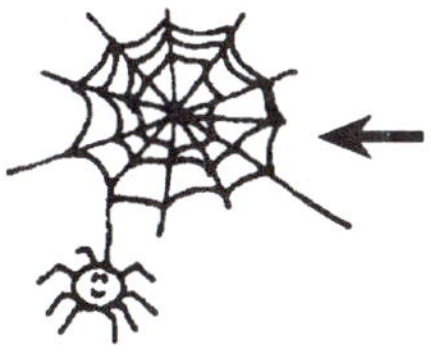
2.	cookout ____________			
3.	drowsy ____________			
4.	workout ____________			
5.	lighthouse ____________		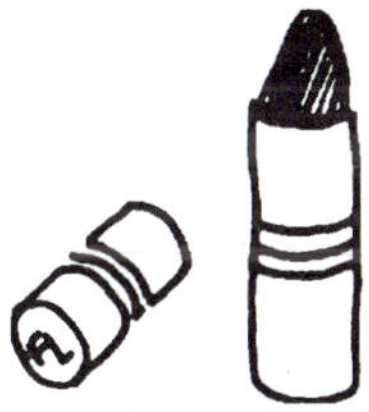	
6.	counting ____________			
7.	cowboy ____________			

 it.

 destroy or downhill?	 downy or drowsy?
 scout or spout?	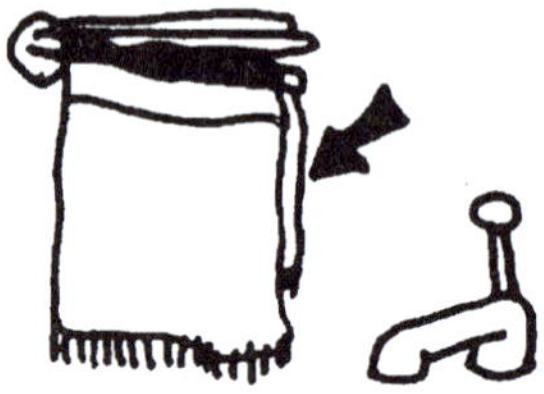 towel or tower?
 scowling or shower?	 couch or coach?
 clouds or clown?	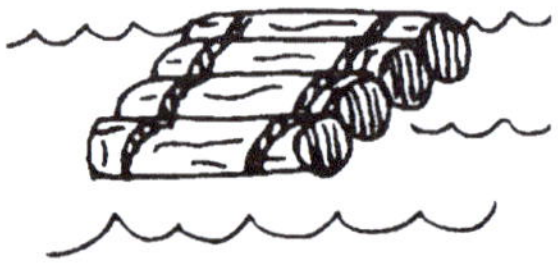 flour or float?
 loudest or proudest?	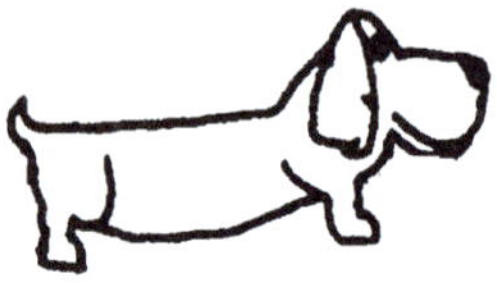 hound or pound?

	Spell.		Write.
1.	 loud cook	out est	________________
2.	 how howl	ing ding	________________
3.	 cloud loud	y er	________________
4.	 scout shout	est ed	________________
5.	 thy thou	sand tend	________________
6.	 show sow	er en	________________
7.	 might night	gain gown	________________

Yes, no, or maybe?

	Question	Yes	No	Maybe
1.	Is a thousand a big amount?	☐	☐	☐
2.	Will a cowgirl powder her horse?	☐	☐	☐
3.	Can you swallow a mouthful of flour?	☐	☐	☐
4.	Do you want a workout when you are drowsy?	☐	☐	☐
5.	Will a cloudy day be the brightest?	☐	☐	☐
6.	Do you live in a crowded townhouse?	☐	☐	☐
7.	Can you hear a wolf howling at the moon at night?	☐	☐	☐

it.

 courting crowning counting	 spouting outing pouting
 tower towel towed	 take a boat! take a bow! take a bowl!
 mouthful mountain mouse hole	 polling plowing blowing
 drowsiness drowning downward	 surround rounded found
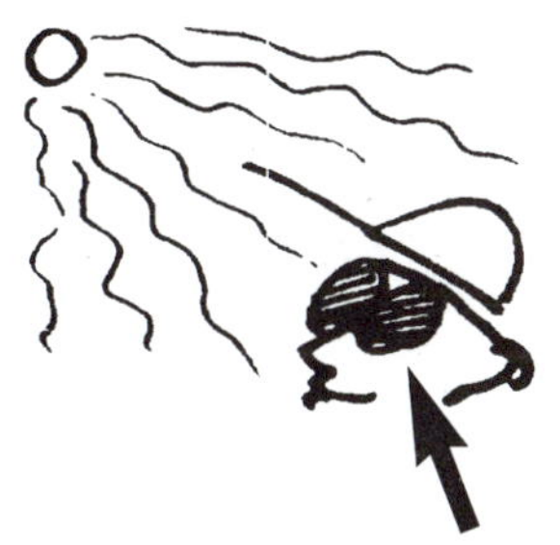 sunflower sunglasses sunscreen	 crowded crowned crowed

Pick the best word to finish each sentence.

shower	drowsy	loudest
thousand	cookout	counting
mouse hole	couch	shouted

1. Do not drive a car when you are feeling__________________.

2. A __________________ is a soft, comfy spot to sit and relax.

3. Nine hundred is less than one __________________.

4. When you are covered with mud, you must take a__________________.

5. Emma is __________________the number of days until her birthday party.

6. He __________________ loudly for his sister to come in the house.

7. That is the__________________ music I have ever heard!

X it.

1.	During the voting we counted a thousand hands.	☐	
	During the countdown we were not allowed to watch.	☐	
2.	The cowboy rounded up the colt and put it in the barn.	☐	
	The cowgirl was around when the colt got out of the barn.	☐	
3.	It is too crowded to swim in the fishbowl.	☐	
	A fishbowl is not a good spot for a clown.	☐	
4.	Sal is counting the mouse holes in his townhouse.	☐	
	Sal is counting on her cats to catch the sly mouse.	☐	
5.	The Texas scouts are rounding up the cows.	☐	
	Tex shouted loudly, but no one heard him.	☐	
6.	The seagull found out he can ride on the tugboat.	☐	
	The tugboat found six gulls riding on the waves.	☐	
7.	Miss Tower is proud of how well Bud reads aloud.	☐	
	Miss Tower is proud of all the buds on her flowers.	☐	

Write it, using a word with **ou** or **ow.**

1.		____________________
2.		____________________
3.		____________________
4.		____________________
5.		____________________
6.		____________________
7.		____________________

Lesson 11

au and **aw** say /aw/ as in h**au**l and s**aw.**

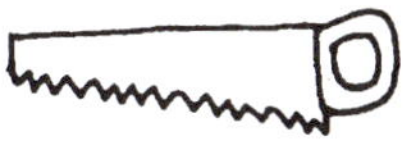

Read, write, and X it.

1.	sprawled ____________		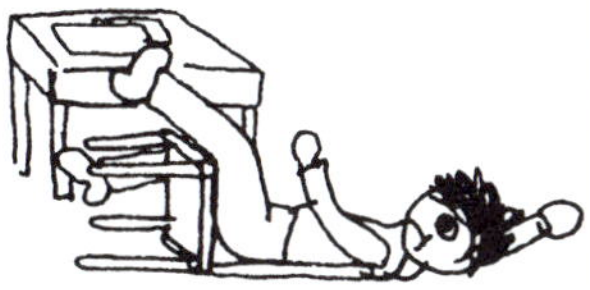	
2.	astronaut ____________		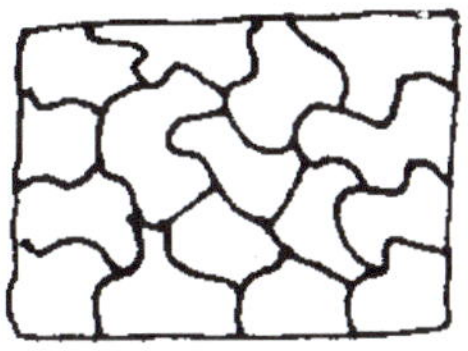	
3.	drawers ____________	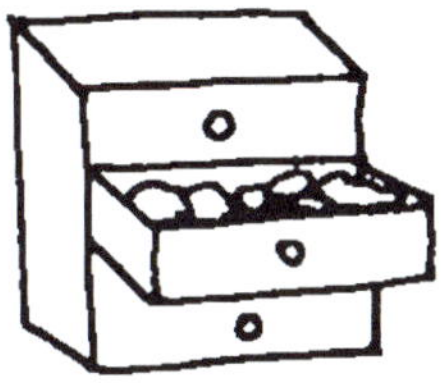		
4.	lawn mower ____________			
5.	shawl ____________			
6.	laundry ____________			
7.	outlaw ____________			

 it.

 yawn or yarn?	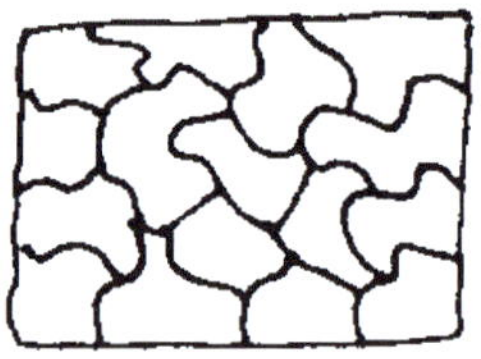 jigsaw or sawbuck?
 raw or row?	 drawing or drowning?
 awful or author?	 taught or tight?
 outlaw or outhouse?	 throwing or thawing?
 hauled or halted?	 laundry or lawmaker?

	Spell.		Write.
1.	 out art	law low	______
2.	 yarn yawn	ing ish	______
3.	 law laun	dry yer	______
4.	 see seen	was saw	______
5.	 audio au	to gram	______
6.	 draw dram	ers ist	______
7.	 au awk	ward thor	______

Yes, no, or maybe?

		Yes	No	Maybe
1.	Do the leaves fall in August?	☐	☐	☐
2.	Can you put together a jigsaw puzzle in the dark?	☐	☐	☐
3.	Do you like coleslaw and raw carrots?	☐	☐	☐
4.	Does the sun set when it is dawn?	☐	☐	☐
5.	Can you put strawberry jam on bread?	☐	☐	☐
6.	Will the snow be thawing in August?	☐	☐	☐
7.	Is it your fault if you break the lawn mower?	☐	☐	☐

◯ it.

strawberry straw hat strawflower	overhasty overcoat overhaul
caught cutest couch	clawed coleslaw crawled
awesome sawdust seesaw	jawbreakers jawbone jailed
daub dawn down	aspirin astronaut automat
somersault summertime sunflower	awning yawning fawning

Pick the best word to finish each sentence.

outlaw	auto	drawers
author	yawning	seesaw
automatic	astronaut	awful

1. A criminal who escapes is an ____________________.

2. It is fun to play with a pal on the ____________________ at the playground.

3. Another nickname for a car is an ____________________.

4. The ____________________ landed safely on the moon.

5. Augie opens the ____________________ of the chest to look for his sweater.

6. ____________________ is something you do when you are sleepy.

7. A camera you do not have to focus is called ____________________.

X it.

1.	Paul skips the trip to the strawberry fields. Paula sips the strawberry shake with a straw. 
2.	The awkward waiter slips and drops the tray. The automatic dumbwaiter carries the trays upstairs. 
3.	Tasha is talking to the lady at the laundry. Tasha is taking down the dry laundry. 
4.	I caught a glimpse of a mouse hiding under the chest. A mouse that loves cheese is apt to get caught. 
5.	Maud gives Otto a tall surprise. Audrey plays lawn tennis at camp. 
6.	Raul wonders what that awful smell might be. Raul wonders why he is such an awful speller. 
7.	Dawn works at sanding and polishing the desk. Todd unplugs the lantern light at dawn. 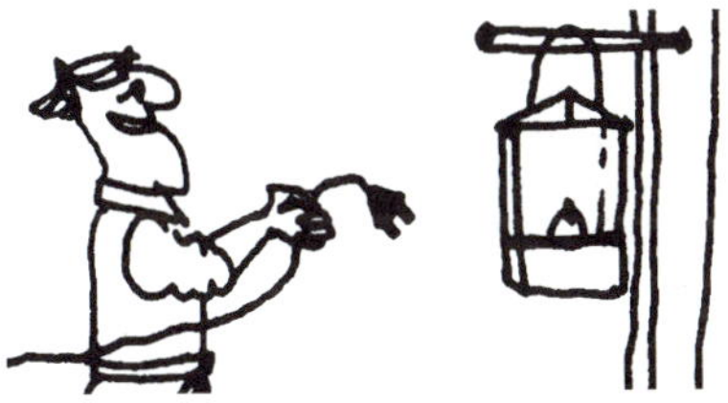

Write it, using a word with **au** or **aw.**

1.		______________________________
2.		______________________________
3.		______________________________
4.		______________________________
5.		______________________________
6.		______________________________
7.		______________________________

Lesson 12

ew, ui, ue, and sometimes **ou** say /ōō/ as in s**ui**t and gl**ue.**

Read, write, and X it.

1.	barbecue ________		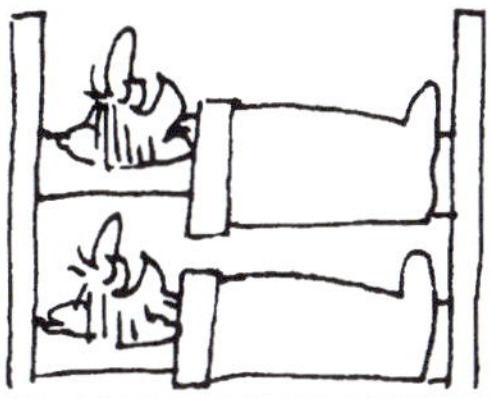	
2.	newspaper ________		 Boston Globe	
3.	bluefish ________			
4.	threw ________			
5.	argue ________			
6.	blue jeans ________		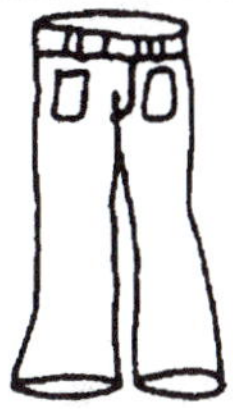	
7.	glue ________			

 it.

 grapefruit or Gatorade?	 newspaper or necktie?
 unglue or undress?	 fruit bowl or fruitcake?
 true story or true love?	 screwball or screwdriver?
 withdrew or worker?	 stewed or statue?
 blue jay or bluefish?	 newlyweds or newsstand?

	Spell.		Write.
1.	 ar or	gue glue	____________
2.	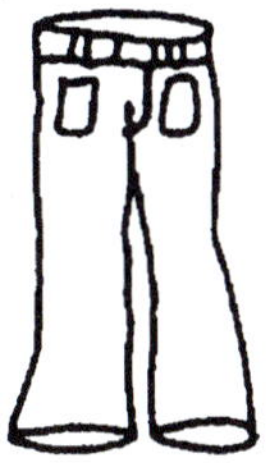 brew blue	fish jeans	____________
3.	 flute fruit	cake coke	____________
4.	 stit stat	ue ing	____________
5.	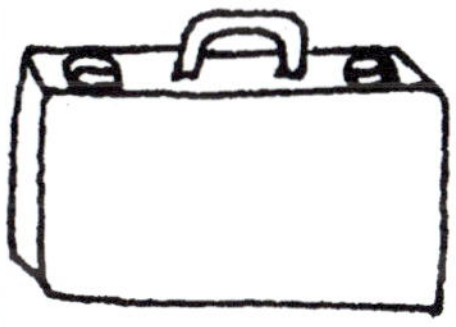 suit sue	case cast	____________
6.	 grap grape	flew fruit	____________
7.	 sap soup	spon spoon	____________

Yes, no, or maybe?

		Yes	No	Maybe
1.	Is a grapefruit bigger than a blueberry?	☐	☐	☐
2.	Can a newspaper be unglued?	☐	☐	☐
3.	If you caught a bluefish, would you throw it back?	☐	☐	☐
4.	If the book is overdue, will you argue about it?	☐	☐	☐
5.	Can a youth group have a barbecue on a cruise boat?	☐	☐	☐
6.	Will a marble statue pack its own suitcase?	☐	☐	☐
7.	Can fruit be bruised?	☐	☐	☐

it.

blueberries
bluebells
bluegrass
stewed
stemmed
strewed
thrive
threw
throat
workmanship
cruise ship
penmanship
glum
glue
glow
yield
youth
yew tree
burn out
blew out
brownout
fruitcake
fruit punch
fruit cup
jeweler
jewelry
weedy
wounded
wooded
wormed

Pick the best word to finish each sentence.

grapefruit	glue	suitcase
statue	threw	chewed
newspapers	overdue	wounded

1. I like to eat half a ____________________ in the morning.

2. To paste things in an album you need sticky ____________________.

3. When you take a trip, you pack your clothes in a ____________________ .

4. Most ____________________ are printed every day.

5. These books are ____________________ at the library.

6. In the park there is a ____________________ of a World War II hero.

7. The pitcher quickly ____________________ the ball to first base.

X it.

1.	The wind blew the shop doors wide open. ☐ The wind blew the group of ships to the New World. ☐	
2.	The crook thinks he can steal some bluefish. ☐ The cook thinks the bluefish stew smells good. ☐	
3.	Sue blew her top when the kids argued. ☐ The top blew off the can and hit Sue. ☐	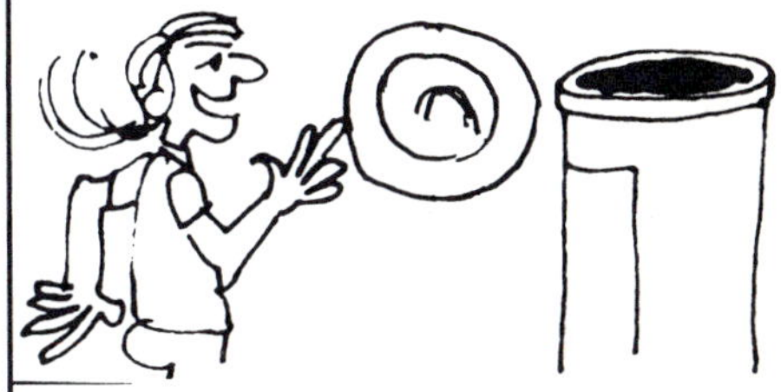
4.	He knew that I really love bluebells! ☐ It's true! Bluebell can read the news! ☐	
5.	The youth tells the queen he worships her. ☐ "Do not argue!" the queen yells at the youth. ☐	
6.	Joon grew up much faster than I knew! ☐ I knew that Stu was a much faster runner than I. ☐	
7.	The third baseman threw the ball and scared the cow. ☐ The scarecrow threw the ball to the outfielder. ☐	

Write it, using a word with **ui, ue, ew,** or **ou.**

1.		
2.		
3.		
4.		
5.		
6.		
7.		

Lesson 13 Review Lesson

Read, write, and X it.

1.	moose ________________			
2.	sprawled ________________			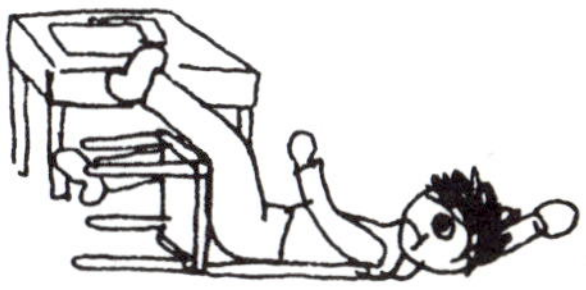
3.	jewelry ________________			
4.	sunflower ________________			
5.	screwdriver ________________			
6.	breathless ________________	 puff		
7.	gorilla ________________			

 it.

 helpless or healthy?	 thawing or throwing?
 moose or mouse?	 cartons or cartoons?
 overhead or overheard?	 raisin or razor?
 worthwhile or workout?	 marshmallow or marmalade?
 sunburned or sunflower?	 ointment or outing?

	Spell.		Write.
1.	 seed sea	house horse	______
2.	 brew blue	berries jeans	______
3.	 tow taw	er el	______
4.	 rea ra	zor sin	______
5.	 bread bead	beard board	______
6.	 heal health	fy y	______
7.	 work walk	up out	______

Yes, no, or maybe?

		Yes	No	Maybe
1.	Is an alley cat a healthy pet?	☐	☐	☐
2.	Can jewelry be worn instead of a kerchief?	☐	☐	☐
3.	Will you do your homework in a high chair?	☐	☐	☐
4.	Are blueberries a tasty treat on top of cornflakes?	☐	☐	☐
5.	Would you keep salad oil in a briefcase?	☐	☐	☐
6.	Will a flounder be found at a cookout?	☐	☐	☐
7.	If you overheard a rumor, would you raise your hand?	☐	☐	☐

 it.

 flowers flounder founder	 hijack highwire high chair
 halted haunted hauled	 launder lawn mower lavender
 screen scowl screw	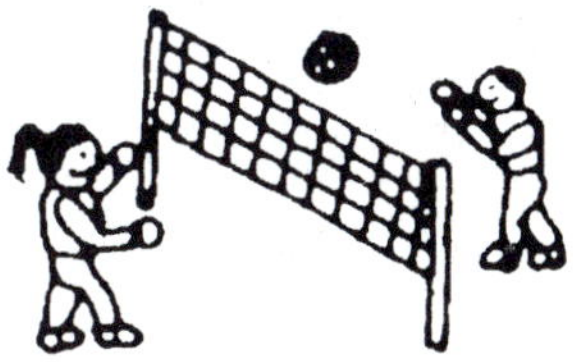 volcano valley volleyball
 arctic arcade armor	 workman workout darkroom
 hosted household hoisted	 hailing howling housing

Pick the best word to finish each sentence.

moose	healthy	blueberries
sunflower	razor	screwdriver
sprawled	hockey	believe

1. On a warm, sunny day it is fun to pick ________________ to make a pie.

2. A big, heavy, deerlike animal with antlers is a ________________.

3. A good diet and a workout every day should keep you ________________.

4. Do you ________________ that Santa Claus is real?

5. Dad uses an electric ________________ when he shaves.

6. You will need a ________________ to take the handle off that door.

7. Most birds at our feeder like ________________ seeds best.

X it.

1.
Maud is the first person in her class to get a learner's permit. ☐

Martha was chilly after she learned to dive off the high board. ☐

2.
Rozell is delighted when she wins tickets to a football game. ☐

Russell squealed with delight when we tickled his foot. ☐

3.
Ricardo raises his hand and shouts the correct answer. ☐

Paulita praises Ricardo for remembering to call home. ☐

4.
Tong is surprised that his chessboard move was not correct. ☐

Latasha surrenders her surfboard to her weeping partner. ☐

5.
Josie waves good-bye as she leaves on the moon launch. ☐

After the year's worst storm the cruise ship is an awful sight. ☐

6.
A warm bathrobe feels cozy when you've had a dreadful day. ☐

Jevon sings loudy as he gets his warm bath ready. ☐

7.
Rachel took a breathful of air and threw herself into the pool. ☐

The hound is breathless from swimming around the pond. ☐

Write it.

1.		
2.		
3.		
4.		
5.		
6.		
7.		

Book 6½ — Posttest

◯ the two words in each box that have the same vowel sound.

1. balloon glue shook	2. beach health steam
3. cry brief flight	4. warmth spark storm
5. caught yawn mouth	6. moist roast most
7. count blows scout	8. lark learn burnt
9. point plow boy	10. score word purse
11. thorn thirst hurt	12. steak beak break

Book 6½ — Posttest

(Teacher dictated. See Key for Book 6½.)

1. underwater underneath unearthed underwear underwent	2. worthy worse worry worst world
3. hearsay heaven healthy headway heavy	4. fielder feeler fielding flier fiesta
5. roosted raised roasted rousted routed	6. throat throw threw thrown threat
7. lightning lightness highness lighting lightest	8. believe belief belie believing believer
9. counts coughs couches coaches catches	10. sprouted spouted sported sparked spawned

Book 6½ — Posttest

(Teacher dictated. See Key for Book 6½.)

1. ______________________________

____

2. ______________________________

____

3. ______________________________

____

4. ______________________________

____

5. ______________________________

____

Book $6^{1}/_{2}$ — Posttest

Use the words to complete the sentences.

outlaws	auto	report
newspaper	underneath	Break!
warned	highway	looking

1. The headline in the ______________ read: PRISON ______________. Printed ______________ the headlines was the story. There had been a riot at the prison and two prisoners escaped. They stole an ______________ and headed out on the expressway. The FBI is now ______________ for the two ______________ on every ______________. They have also ______________ people to be on the lookout and to ______________ any sight of them.

jockey	horseback	willpower
pounds	shorter	worthwhile
thousand	heavy	high

2. To become a ______________ requires many things. First of all, you must be ______________ than most people and not too ______________. The smallest jockey in history weighed in at only 49 ______________. Skill in riding ______________ at ______________ speeds takes much time and hard work with one's horse. It also requires firmness and ______________ to stick with this task. But the reward of a purse of over ninety ________________ dollars makes it all ______________.

shouted	August	loudest
pointing	fireworks	brightest
noisy	ballfield	backward

3. Last July 4 our town had a grand ______________ display. The event was held at the school ______________. As the rockets were bursting, everyone began ______________. "Look at that! WOW!" we all exclaimed. But the show was also a bit frightening. The loud, shrill sound followed by the popping and shower of sparks was startling. Stunned, I looked up and started walking backward to see the lights better. My pal ______________ at me to watch out, but too late! I tripped, fell over ________________, and landed in a mud puddle. Those fireworks were the ________________, and the ______________, *and* the muddiest I have ever seen!